Contents

A note on Nathaniel Hawthorne   5
Introduction   8

Young Goodman Brown

PART ONE   A Mysterious Forest   11
PART TWO   A Terrifying Discovery   24

ACTIVITIES   18, 31

New England and witchcraft   34

The Birthmark

PART ONE   A Beautiful Young Woman   43
PART TWO   Perfection is Dangerous   54

ACTIVITIES   50, 60

The magic of alchemy   63

Dr Heidegger's Experiment

PART **ONE**	Dr Heidegger's Friends	69
PART **TWO**	The Fountain of Youth	80

ACTIVITIES	75, 87
INTERNET PROJECT	39
EXIT TEST	92
KEY TO **EXIT TEST**	96

	Cambridge **P**reliminary **E**nglish **T**est-style exercises
T: GRADE 5	Trinity-style exercises (Grade 5)

This story is recorded in full.

 These symbols indicate the beginning and end of the extracts linked to the listening activities.

Nathaniel Hawthorne

Stories of Suspense

Retold by **Gina D. B. Clemen**
Activities by **Matt Renzi**

Editors: Emma Berridge, Rebecca Raynes
Design and art direction: Nadia Maestri
Computer graphics: Simona Corniola
Illustrations: Anna and Elena Balbusso
Picture research: Laura Lagomarsino

© 2004   Black Cat Publishing,
           an imprint of Cideb Editrice, Genoa, Canterbury

First edition: May 2004

Picture credits:
National Portrait Gallery, Smithsonian Institution / Art Resource NY: 5; Library of Congress, Prints and Photographs Division, Washington: 8; The Granger Collection, New York: 34, 35; photograph courtesy of the Peabody Essex Museum: 36; Musée de Tesse, Le Mans, France / Lauros / Giraudon / Bridgeman Art Library: 63; British Library, London, UK / Bridgeman Art Library: 65

All rights reserved. No part of this book may be reproduced, stored in a retrieval system, or transmitted, in any form or by any means, electronic, mechanical, photocopying, recording or otherwise, without the written permission of the publisher.

We would be happy to receive your comments and suggestions, and give you any other information concerning our material.
editorial@blackcat-cideb.com
www.blackcat-cideb.com
www.cideb.it

ISBN 88-530-0159-3   Book
ISBN 88-530-0160-7   Book + CD

Printed in Italy

Nathaniel Hawthorne (1862) by Emanuel Gottlieb Leutze.

A note on
Nathaniel Hawthorne

Nathaniel Hawthorne was born in Salem, Massachusetts, on July 4, 1804. One of his ancestors was William Hathorne (Nathaniel Hawthorne added the "w"), who came to the New World in 1630 with the first Puritans. Hathorne's son John was a judge at the Salem witch trials in 1692 (see the dossier on page 34).

Nathaniel Hawthorne was very interested in his Puritan ancestors, their way of life and their strict religion. But he was almost ashamed of [1] what they had done during the Salem witch trials.

---

1. **ashamed of** : embarassed or guilty about.

Witchcraft is a common theme in Hawthorne's works. He was fascinated by the history and legends of Salem and Boston, as you can see in his short stories.

Hawthorne attended Bowdoin College in Maine and decided to become a writer. In 1837 he published a collection of short stories, *Twice-Told Tales*. "Dr Heidegger's Experiment" is part of this collection. In 1842 he married Sophia Peabody. They had three children.

He published another collection of short stories in 1846, *Mosses from an Old Manse*. "Young Goodman Brown" and "The Birthmark" are included in this collection.

He worked at the Salem Custom House from 1846-9, when he began writing his famous novel *The Scarlet Letter*. It was published in 1850 and is considered his masterpiece.

The House of the Seven Gables was published in 1851, and *The Blithedale Romance* in 1852.

Hawthorne left for England in 1853 where he was appointed U.S. Consul in Liverpool and Manchester. While he was in England he traveled to France and Italy. He wrote his last novel, *The Marble Faun*, in Italy, although it was published in the United States in 1860.

He died on May 19, 1864 and left several unfinished works. Hawthorne is considered one of America's greatest writers because of his vivid imagination and deep psychological understanding of his characters.

PET ① Look at the sentences below about Nathaniel Hawthorne. Decide if each sentence is correct or incorrect. If it is correct, write A as your answer. If it is not correct, write B as your answer.

1. Nathaniel Hawthorne was born in Salem, Massachusetts.
2. He wasn't interested in Puritanism.
3. *The Scarlet Letter* is one of his most famous books.
4. Hawthorne was interested in the history of Salem and Boston.
5. He had four children.
6. Hawthorne was appointed U.S. consul in Liverpool and Manchester.
7. While living in Boston he traveled to France and Italy.
8. His last novel was written in France.
9. He left no unfinished works.
10. He is considered one of America's greatest authors.

1 ......   2 ......   3 ......   4 ......   5 ......
6 ......   7 ......   8 ......   9 ......   10 ......

Now read the text again and correct the incorrect statements.

② Match the important events in Hawthorne's life with the corresponding year(s). Write the event or year below.

Event	Year(s)
a. Nathaniel Hawthorne was born	
b.	1837
c. Hawthorne married Sophia Peabody	
d. *Mosses from an Old Manse* was published	
e.	1846-9
f.	1850
g. *The House of the Seven Gables* was published	
h.	1853
i. Nathaniel Hawthorne died	

Introduction

The three short stories you will read take place in New England, where Hawthorne was born and lived. There is something eerie [1] and mysterious in each story. Hawthorne studied the history and legends of the Puritans and their ancestors. They were obsessed with witchcraft, [2] evil [3] and the devil.
You will see this particularly as you read "Young Goodman Brown".

Boston (*c.* 1833) by William James Bennet.

1. **eerie** : strange and frightening.
2. **witchcraft** : the use of magic powers.
3. **evil** : bad things.

Young Goodman Brown

ACTIVITIES

Before you read

1 Listen to the beginning of Part One. Decide if each sentence is correct or incorrect. If it is correct, put a tick (✓) in the box under A for YES. If it is not correct, put a tick (✓) in the box under B for NO.

		A YES	B NO
1	Faith wore blue ribbons in her hair.	☐	☐
2	Faith wanted Goodman Brown to make the journey.	☐	☐
3	Goodman Brown told Faith to stay awake and wait for him to return.	☐	☐
4	Faith was unhappy when she spoke to Goodman Brown.	☐	☐
5	Goodman Brown took a dark road through the forest.	☐	☐
6	Goodman Brown wasn't frightened at all when he walked alone in the forest.	☐	☐
7	On the road in front of him, Goodman Brown met a man who sat under a tree.	☐	☐
8	Goodman Brown was early for the appointment.	☐	☐
9	The man and Goodman Brown looked very similar.	☐	☐
10	The man carried a staff which looked like a snake.	☐	☐

Now read the text and correct the incorrect sentences.

PART **ONE**

A Mysterious Forest

At sunset Young Goodman [1] Brown stepped into the street of Salem village. But then he put his head back inside his house and kissed his young wife Faith. She put her pretty head outside the house. The wind played with the pink ribbons [2] in her hair while she called her husband.

"Dearest love," she said, "please leave in the morning and sleep in your own bed tonight. Please stay with me tonight, dear husband."

1. **Goodman** : Puritan expression for a married man.
2. **ribbons** :

Stories of *Suspense*

"My love and my Faith," answered young Goodman Brown, "tonight I must stay away from you. I must make this journey between now and sunrise."

"I will wait for you to return," said Faith, with her pink ribbons.

"Say your prayers,[1] dear Faith, and go to bed early, then nothing will happen to you."

The young man walked on and then looked back. He saw Faith's head with her pink ribbons. She was still looking at him.

"Poor little Faith!" he thought. "I should not leave her alone while I go on this journey. She often talks of dreams. When she spoke to me there was unhappiness in her face. Perhaps a dream told her what I am doing tonight! Oh, but it will kill her to think of it. She is an angel, and after tonight I will stay close to her forever."

With this excellent resolution for the future, Goodman Brown felt better. He walked quickly toward his evil purpose.[2] He took a dark, mysterious road in the forest with tall, dark trees all around him. It was very lonely and he did not know what was hidden behind the dark trees.

"There could be an Indian behind every tree," said Goodman Brown to himself. He was afraid. He looked behind him and said, "What if the devil is here?"

On the road in front of him there was a man sitting under an old tree. He got up and said, "You are late, Goodman Brown."

Surprised by his sudden appearance, he replied nervously, "I was with Faith."

---

1. **prayers** : the activity of speaking to God.
2. **evil purpose** : bad or wrong intention.

Young GOODMAN BROWN

It was now very dark in the forest. The second traveler was about fifty years old and looked a lot like Goodman Brown. They looked like father and son. But, although the older man was simply dressed, he had a certain air of one who knew the world. He would be comfortable at the governor's table or at King William's court. But the only unusual thing about him was his staff.[1] It was a strange staff. It looked like a living serpent. Of course, it was probably Goodman Brown's imagination because it was very dark in the forest.

"Come, Goodman Brown," cried his fellow traveler. "You are walking too slowly. Take my staff if you are tired."

"My friend," said Goodman Brown, stopping, "I met you here because I promised. But now I want to return home because I am worried about this journey."

"Really?" replied the older companion. "Let us walk on. If I can convince you while we walk, then you must not go back. And if I cannot convince you, then you can go back. We have just entered the forest."

Goodman Brown started walking again. "My father never went to the forest on such a journey, and neither did his father before him. We are a family of honest men and good Christians. I will be the first Brown that ever took this path in the forest and had—"

"And had such friends. That's what you wanted to say," said the older man. "I have known your family very well. I knew your grandfather and your father. I helped your grandfather when he whipped[2] the Quaker woman in Salem. And I helped him to burn

---

1. **staff**: a long piece of wood. 2. **whipped**: hit with a whip.

an Indian village. They were my good friends and we walked along this path many times and returned after midnight."

"I am surprised that they never spoke about these things. But I can understand why. We are a people of prayer and work, and we do not tolerate evil."

"Evil or not," said the traveler with the staff, "I know many important people here in New England — religious men, government officials and the governor himself!"

"Really?" cried Goodman Brown. "I don't know the governor or government officials. But if I continue this journey, how can I meet the eye of that good old man, our minister at Salem village? His voice will make me tremble."

Until now the older traveler had listened seriously, but he suddenly started laughing loudly. He laughed violently and his serpent-like staff seemed to move.

"Ha! ha! ha!" he shouted again and again. Then he said, "Well, go on, Goodman Brown, go on. But please don't kill me with laughing."

"To end the discussion," said Goodman Brown, angrily, "there is my wife Faith. It will break her dear little heart."

"If that is the case," answered the other, "then go home, Goodman Brown. I don't want anything bad to happen to Faith."

On the path in front of them they saw an old lady who had taught Goodman Brown catechism when he was a child. She was still his spiritual teacher, together with the minister and Deacon Gookin.

"How strange that Goody [1] Cloyse is in the forest tonight," said Goodman Brown. "With your permission, my friend, I will

---

1. **Goody** : Puritan expression for a married woman.

Stories of Suspense

take another path through the woods and leave this Christian woman behind. I don't want to meet her. She may ask me where I am going."

"Very well," said the older traveler. "You go on through the woods and I will walk on the path."

The young man turned into the woods but watched his companion who walked along the path. The old lady was walking along quickly for a woman of her age. The traveler touched her neck with his staff.

"The devil!" screamed the old lady.

"It's your old friend," said the traveler.

"Ah, of course, it is you, your worship! [1] Yes, it is really you and in the image of Goodman Brown's grandfather," cried the old woman. "Well, I was ready for the meeting but I had no horse to ride on. My broomstick [2] has disappeared. I think the witch Goody Cory stole it. So I decided to come on foot. If you give me your arm we will be there shortly."

"I cannot give you my arm," answered her friend, "but here is my staff."

He threw it on the ground and Goodman Brown thought that the staff took the form of a serpent, but he wasn't sure. First he looked up and then he looked down, and he did not see Goody Cloyse or the serpent-like staff. All he saw was his fellow traveler [3] who was waiting for him calmly.

---

1. **your worship** : (here) title of great respect used for a supernatural being, in this case the devil.
2. **broomstick** :
3. **fellow traveler** : the person traveling with him.

Young GOODMAN BROWN

"That old woman taught me catechism," said young Goodman Brown. And there was a world of meaning in that simple comment.

They continued walking in the forest and talking. The older traveler broke the branch of a tree and used it as a walking staff. Suddenly Goodman Brown sat down under a tree and refused to continue.

"My friend," he said, "I have decided that the horrible old woman can go to the devil if she wants. I always thought she wanted to go to heaven. That is not a reason to leave my dear Faith and follow her."

The older traveler said calmly, "Sit here and rest. When you want to continue, here is my staff to help you."

He threw his companion the staff and disappeared into the dark forest. Goodman Brown sat there for a few moments. He was proud of [1] himself because he had a clean conscience and he could look Deacon Gookin straight in the eye. And that night he could sleep in Faith's arms, instead of spending the night in the forest. As he was thinking these pleasant thoughts, he heard the sound of horses along the path. He decided to hide in the forest.

1. **proud of** : satisfied with, pleased with.

Go back to the text

1 **Choose the correct answer (a, b, c or d) to the questions below.**

1. When did Goodman Brown have to make his journey?
   a. ☐ at sunrise
   b. ☐ at night
   c. ☐ in the morning
   d. ☐ at sunset

2. What did Goodman Brown think was behind every tree in the forest?
   a. ☐ witches
   b. ☐ Indians
   c. ☐ demons
   d. ☐ Faith

3. Which statement is *not* true about Goodman Brown's companion?
   a. ☐ He knew many important people in New England.
   b. ☐ He carried a staff which looked like a serpent.
   c. ☐ He looked similar to Brown.
   d. ☐ He carried a broomstick.

4. Which word would *not* describe Goodman Brown's family?
   a. ☐ honest
   b. ☐ hard-working
   c. ☐ religious
   d. ☐ humorous

ACTIVITIES

5. Who was Goody Cloyse?
   a. ☐ Goodman Brown's old catechism teacher
   b. ☐ a friend of Faith's
   c. ☐ a Quaker woman who lived in Salem
   d. ☐ King William's daughter

6. Why did Goodman Brown take another path?
   a. ☐ Because he didn't want to meet Goody Cloyse.
   b. ☐ Because he was afraid.
   c. ☐ Because he remembered his dream.
   d. ☐ Because he saw Deacon Gookin.

7. According to Goody Cloyse, who did the traveler look like?
   a. ☐ Goodman Brown's father
   b. ☐ Goodman Brown's grandfather
   c. ☐ Deacon Gookin
   d. ☐ Goody Cory

8. Why was Goodman Brown proud of himself?
   a. ☐ Because he had a clean conscience.
   b. ☐ Because he went to church every Sunday.
   c. ☐ Because he was a Puritan.
   d. ☐ Because he had a beautiful wife named Faith.

9. Why did Goodman Brown hide in the forest?
   a. ☐ Because he was scared of Goody Cloyse.
   b. ☐ Because his companion told him to.
   c. ☐ Because he heard the sound of horses.
   d. ☐ Because he didn't want to return home.

ACTIVITIES

PET 2 Read the text below about Nathaniel Hawthorne's home and choose the correct word for each space. For each question, write the correct letter, A, B, C or D.

Located **(1)** ………. Concord, Massachusetts, "The Wayside" was the only home that Nathaniel Hawthorne ever owned. In **(2)** ………., although Hawthorne is one of America's greatest writers, he was not **(3)** ………. wealthy. "The Wayside" is also the only National Historic Landmark **(4)** ………. in by three literary families.

Before Hawthorne bought **(5)** ………., the house belonged **(6)** ………. the Alcott family, **(7)** ………. named it "Hillside". Here, Louisa May Alcott and her sisters lived much of the childhood **(8)** ………. in the classic novel, *Little Women*.

When Hawthorne bought it, he changed the name to "The Wayside".

Now part of Minute Man National Historical Park, "The Wayside" **(9)** ………. preserved by children's author Margaret Sidney, **(10)** ………. of the "Five Little Peppers", and **(11)** ………. daughter, Margaret Lothrop. In 1924, Lothrop inherited "The Wayside" and devoted her life to saving the "Home of Authors" **(12)** ………. her death in May, 1970.

1	A by	B on	C in	D of
2	A fact	B truth	C true	D facts
3	A so	B all	C too	D particularly
4	A live	B living	C lived	D lives
5	A it	B that	C those	D them
6	A for	B to	C of	D with
7	A who	B that	C whose	D who's
8	A describing	B describes	C described	D describe
9	A was	B were	C has	D is
10	A create	B creator	C creating	D creation
11	A her	B she	C it's	D hers
12	A when	B until	C then	D and

ACTIVITIES

PET 3 Look at the text in each question. What does it say? Mark the correct letter A, B or C.

1. MEETING TONIGHT AT 7.00. NO ADMITTANCE AFTER 7.15

   A ☐ If you arrive after 7.15 you can't come in.
   B ☐ The meeting will be later than usual.
   C ☐ The meeting starts at 7.15.

2. PEDESTRIANS ONLY. NO BICYCLES ON PATH

   A ☐ Only bicycles can use this path.
   B ☐ Pedestrians aren't allowed on this path.
   C ☐ You can't bring bicycles on this path.

3. WARNING: NO FEEDING ANIMALS IN FOREST

   A ☐ You aren't allowed to give food to the animals.
   B ☐ Animals aren't allowed in the forest.
   C ☐ Animals can't eat in the forest.

4. REWARD! $100 for lost broomstick. If found please CALL: 555-5555

   A ☐ If you lost a broomstick, call 555-5555.
   B ☐ You will receive money if you find the broomstick.
   C ☐ If you call 555-5555, you will receive $100.

5. Silence in the church please, people are praying

   A ☐ It's quiet in the church.
   B ☐ Don't talk in the church.
   C ☐ You must pray very quietly.

ACTIVITIES

Before you read

PET 1 Listen to the beginning of Part Two. For each question, put a tick (✓) in the correct box.

1 Why didn't Goodman Brown recognize the men on horses?
   - A ☐ Because they were wearing masks.
   - B ☐ Because it was too dark.
   - C ☐ Because he was too tired.

2 Whose voice did Goodman Brown think he heard?
   - A ☐ the Deacon's
   - B ☐ Faith's
   - C ☐ his father's

3 Who *wasn't* going to the meeting that night?
   - A ☐ Indian men of magic
   - B ☐ a lovely young woman
   - C ☐ an old couple from California

4 What sounds filled the night?
   - A ☐ cries of anger and terror
   - B ☐ laughter and jokes
   - C ☐ terrible screams and banging sounds

5 According to Goodman Brown, who did "this world belong to?"
   - A ☐ God
   - B ☐ the devil
   - C ☐ Mother Nature

ACTIVITIES

6 What happened to Goodman Brown as he continued walking along the road?
  A ☐ It became darker and more frightening.
  B ☐ It became lighter and easier to see.
  C ☐ He became frightened and went home.

7 As Brown continued along the road, what did he hear?
  A ☐ a chorus of human voices
  B ☐ trees falling
  C ☐ horses running

8 What was there around the altar?
  A ☐ many people
  B ☐ horses
  C ☐ burning trees

9 What was interesting about the group of people?
  A ☐ There were good as well as bad people.
  B ☐ They were all important people.
  C ☐ They were all criminals.

10 Who were the people singing to?
  A ☐ an angel
  B ☐ the devil
  C ☐ the animals of the forest

Now read the text and check your answers.

PART **TWO**

A Terrifying Discovery

Goodman Brown did not recognize the men on the horses because it was too dark. However, he thought he heard the voices of the minister and Deacon Gookin.

The voice that sounded like the Deacon's said, "I can't miss tonight's meeting! There will be people of our community from Falmouth and others from Connecticut and Rhode Island. And there will be Indian men of magic who know a lot about devilry. There will also be a lovely young woman who will join our group."

"Very well, Deacon Gookin!" replied the old minister. "Let us go quickly. We must not be late."

Young GOODMAN BROWN

The horses galloped through the forest. Goodman Brown was very surprised and his heart was heavy. He looked up at the sky to see if there was a heaven above him. He saw the sky and the bright stars.

"With heaven above and Faith below, I will resist the devil!" cried Goodman Brown.

While he looked up at the sky and prayed, he saw a black cloud directly above him. From the black cloud he heard the sound of confused voices. They sounded like the voices of his own townspeople. Then he heard the sad voice of a young woman.

"Faith!" shouted Goodman Brown, who was very worried. And the forest echoed "Faith! Faith!"

The cries of anger and terror filled the night. Then there were sounds of other voices, terrible screams and laughter. The black cloud passed over his head and something fell down slowly — it was a pink ribbon.

"My Faith is gone!" he cried. "Oh, there is no good in this world. This world belongs to the devil."

Young Goodman Brown was desperate. He took his staff and started walking very quickly. The road became darker and more frightening. There were strange, terrible sounds everywhere.

"Ha! ha! ha!" cried Goodman Brown when the wind laughed at him. "You can't frighten me! Come witch, come wizard, [1] come the devil himself — here comes Goodman Brown. He's not afraid of you!"

In all the mysterious forest the figure of Goodman Brown was the most frightening. He went forward courageously as he listened to a strange chorus of human voices.

1. **wizard** : a man who has magic powers.

Stories of Suspense

Then suddenly he reached an opening in the forest. The opening looked like an altar. It was surrounded by burning trees that looked like candles. The red light of the fire was everywhere.

"What a strange group!" said Goodman Brown.

In this group there were ministers, church members of Salem village, pious [1] ladies, important men of the government and young girls. Good old Deacon Gookin was there too. However, among these good people there were also thieves, criminals and bad people. They were all together.

"But where is Faith?" thought Goodman Brown nervously.

He heard a hymn. It was a slow, sad hymn about dark sins [2] and evil. The chorus sang and a loud organ played. Everyone was singing to the devil. It was an image of horror!

Then suddenly a voice cried, "Bring in the converts!"

When he heard this Goodman Brown approached the group and he felt evil. He thought he saw his dead father calling him. Then he saw a sad woman who put out her hand to warn [3] him. Was she his mother? Then the old minister and Deacon Gookin took his arm and brought him forward.

A thin woman with a veil on her face walked between Goody Cloyse, the pious catechism teacher, and Martha Carrier, an evil woman. Martha Carrier wanted to become the queen of hell. The converts stood there surrounded by the fire.

"Welcome, my children," said the dark figure. "You have now found your true nature and your destiny. My children, look behind you!"

1. **pious** : with strong religious beliefs.
2. **sins** : disobedience to the laws of religion.
3. **warn** : tell of something bad that may happen.

Young GOODMAN BROWN

They turned around and saw the fire. There was a strange smile on every dark face.

"All the people you knew and respected are here. You thought they were better than you, but they are all here worshipping me," said the dark figure. "Tonight you will know all their darkest secrets. You will know that respected men of the church have said evil words to young girls, that pious women have poisoned their husbands and that young men have killed their fathers to get their money. You will understand the mystery of sin and evil. And now, my children, look at each other."

They all looked at each other. Suddenly Goodman Brown saw Faith and she saw her husband.

"Remember, evil is the nature of all people. Evil must be your only happiness. Welcome again, my children."

"Welcome," repeated the devil worshippers.[1]

Young Goodman Brown and Faith stood among the others. They seemed undecided. Did they want to go on? Goodman Brown looked at his wife and she looked at him.

"Faith! Faith!" cried Goodman Brown. "Look up to heaven and resist the devil."

He did not know if Faith obeyed him. After he had spoken he found himself alone, with the sound of the wind in the forest. He was standing against a cold, humid rock. A branch of a tree that had been on fire was now cold and wet.

***

1. **devil worshippers** : people who believe in the devil.

Stories of *Suspense*

The next morning young Goodman Brown walked slowly in Salem village. He was a very confused man. He saw the good minister walking near the cemetery and preparing his sermon. Goodman Brown avoided [1] the old man. Old Deacon Gookin was praying and Goodman Brown could hear his prayers through the open window.

"Who is he praying to?" thought Goodman Brown. Goody Cloyse, the pious old Christian, was giving religious instruction to a little girl. Goodman Brown pulled the little girl away. Near the church he saw Faith's head with the pretty pink ribbons. She was very happy to see her husband and almost kissed him in front of the whole village. But Goodman Brown looked at her severely and sadly, and walked on.

Did Goodman Brown fall asleep in the forest and only have a terrible dream about a witch meeting and the devil?

Perhaps, but it was a dream of evil omen [2] for young Goodman Brown. After that strange night he became a sad, dark, almost desperate man.

On Sunday when the congregation sang a hymn, he could not listen to it. He could still hear the frightening hymn of the night in the forest. At night he often awoke and moved away from Faith. When the family prayed he looked at them angrily and turned away.

After a long life, Goodman Brown's body was carried to his grave followed by Faith, his children and grandchildren. There was a procession with many friends, but there were no hopeful words on his tombstone because his last hour was very sad and hopeless.

1. **avoided** : stayed away from.
2. **omen** : a sign that something is going to happen in the future.

A C T I V I T I E S

Go back to the text

PET ① Look at the sentences below about Part Two. Decide if each sentence is correct or incorrect. If it is correct, write A as your answer. If it is not correct, write B as your answer.

1 Goodman Brown saw a black cloud directly above him while he was praying.
2 A pink ribbon fell down from the sky.
3 In the opening in the forest Goodman Brown only saw a group of thieves and criminals.
4 Goodman Brown thought the group was very strange.
5 Goodman Brown thought he saw his father trying to warn him.
6 Martha Carrier was an evil woman who wanted to become the queen of hell.
7 The morning after the ceremony Goodman Brown wanted to see Deacon Gookin.
8 Goodman Brown didn't know if his experience the night before in the forest was a dream.
9 Goodman Brown remained a happy man even after his strange night in the forest.
10 When Goodman Brown died, kind words were written on his tombstone.

1 ......   2 ......   3 ......   4 ......   5 ......
6 ......   7 ......   8 ......   9 ......   10 ......

ACTIVITIES

"After a long life, Goodman Brown's body was carried to his grave"

We use a passive verb to say what happens to the subject.

To form the passive, we use a form of the verb **to be** + **the past participle**.

Look at these examples:
Someone stole her bag yesterday.
*Her bag **was stolen** yesterday.*
Past Simple of to be + past participle

We can use **by** after the passive verb when we want to show who the agent is:
The mechanic repaired my car last week.
*My car was repaired **by** the mechanic last week.*

2 Change the sentences below to the passive form in the Past Simple or Present Simple.

a. Goodman Brown left Faith alone for the night.
   Faith ....

b. The voices in the forest frightened Goodman Brown.
   Goodman Brown ....

c. After midnight they brought in all the converts.
   The converts ....

d. All the participants sang hymns at the meeting.
   Hymns ....

e. The people of Salem respected young Goodman Brown.
   Young Goodman Brown ....

f. Nobody wrote hopeful words on Goodman Brown's tombstone.
   No hopeful words ....

g. Hawthorne wrote "Young Goodman Brown" in 1835.
   "Young Goodman Brown" ....

h. People consider Hawthorne one of the greatest American writers.
   Hawthorne ....

ACTIVITIES

3 Let's talk about the story.
Answer the questions below in your own words, then ask your classmates what they think.

  a. Who do you think the dark figure in the forest was?
     Can the dark figure be any other of the characters in the story?
  b. What did Goodman Brown learn in the forest?
  c. Why do you think Goodman Brown didn't speak to the people of the town the next day?
  d. Why do you think Goodman Brown's "last hour was very sad and hopeless"?
  e. Why do you think Hawthorne called Goodman Brown's wife Faith?

PET 4 Have you ever had a strange or eerie experience? Write a story about what happened. Your story must begin with this sentence:

> I'll never forget the strange thing that happened to me.

Write your story in about 100 words.

T: GRADE 5

5 Topic — Festivals
Which festival do you think of when you hear the words "witch", "wizard", "frightening", "afraid", "horror", and "evil"?
Prepare a talk for the class about Halloween. Bring in a photo or object that reminds you of Halloween. Use the questions below to help you prepare your talk.

  a. Describe your photo or object.
  b. What do you know about Halloween?
  c. Have you ever been to a Halloween celebration?
  d. If it's not Halloween, what is your favorite celebration?

New England and *witchcraft*

The early settlers [1] of Salem and Boston, in the area which became known as New England, were Puritans. The Puritans left England for America in 1620 because they were persecuted for their religious beliefs. They wanted to practice their religion freely in the New World. Every part of their life was influenced by their religion. They wore black and dark gray clothes and observed strict morality. They believed in hard work, thrift [2] and honesty. People who did not obey the teachings of the church were severely punished.

The pillory – a form of punishment used by the Puritans (19th century).

1. **settlers** : people who come to live permanently in a new country.
2. **thrift** : using their money very carefully.

Persons accused of witchcraft were hanged [1] or burned. Puritans believed that witches were in contact with the devil and other evil spirits. They believed that they had supernatural powers.

In 1692 in Salem a few adolescent girls listened to the strange stories of Tituba, a slave girl from the West Indies. Suddenly these girls began acting very strangely – they made animal noises, jumped around and threw themselves to the ground. The town doctor said that they were bewitched. [2] The girls accused Tituba and two other white women of being witches.

The "witch" Tituba of Salem (19th century).

1. **hanged**:
2. **bewitched** : possessed by the devil.

All the people in Salem believed that the devil was among them. The terrible witchcraft trials began. The "bewitched girls" began accusing many people in the town. Soon the Salem prison was full of men, women and children. They were all accused of witchcraft. Important Puritan magistrates listened to these people at the trials which continued for many months.

After ten months, nineteen people were hanged and more than one hundred were put in prison. Others died in prison before they could be tried.

Soon people outside of Salem were accused of witchcraft. Even the governor's wife and a Puritan reverend were accused. The magistrates decided that something was wrong. After a year the

Examination of a witch (1855) by Thomas H. Matteson.

terrible witch-hunt [1] was finally over. After Salem, there were no more witch-hunts in the United States. However, during the 18th century witches were still burned in Europe.

Today you can visit the famous Salem Witch Museum in Salem, where you can find out all about Salem's history and the witch trials (see the Internet Project, page 39).

1 Choose the correct answer (a, b, c or d) to the questions below.

1. Why did the early settlers of Salem and Boston leave England?
   a. ☐ Because they were persecuted for their religious beliefs.
   b. ☐ Because they were curious about the "new land".
   c. ☐ Because they were bored in England.
   d. ☐ Because they owed money to the government.

2. Which statement is *not* true about the early settlers?
   a. ☐ They dressed in black and dark gray.
   b. ☐ They were hard-working people.
   c. ☐ They were honest people.
   d. ☐ They spent all their money on unnecessary things.

3. What happened to people who were accused of witchcraft?
   a. ☐ They were hanged or burned.
   b. ☐ They were sent away.
   c. ☐ They were sent to prison.
   d. ☐ They were released.

1. **witch-hunt** : search to find and punish people thought to be witches.

4. Who was Tituba?
   a. ☐ the town doctor
   b. ☐ a slave girl
   c. ☐ a Puritan reverend's wife
   d. ☐ a witch

5. What *didn't* the girls do when they heard Tituba's stories?
   a. ☐ They made animal sounds.
   b. ☐ They acted strangely.
   c. ☐ They threw themselves to the ground.
   d. ☐ They started stealing things.

6. How many people were hanged during the Salem Witch Trials?
   a. ☐ four
   b. ☐ ten
   c. ☐ nineteen
   d. ☐ one hundred

7. Which statement is *false*?
   a. ☐ The Governor's wife of Salem was accused of being a witch.
   b. ☐ People outside of Salem were accused of witchcraft.
   c. ☐ After Salem, there were two more witch-hunts in the United States.
   d. ☐ A Puritan reverend was accused of witchcraft.

8. How long did the witch-hunt last?
   a. ☐ one year
   b. ☐ one month
   c. ☐ two years
   d. ☐ one day

INTERNET PROJECT

Find out about life in Salem!

What was life like in Salem during the famous witch trials? Find the information you need to answer the questions on page 40.

Connect to the Internet and go to www.blackcat-cideb.com or www.cideb.it. Insert the title or part of the title of the book into our search engine. Open the page for *Stories of Suspense*. Click on the project link symbol . Go down the page until you find the title of this book and click on the link with the symbol .

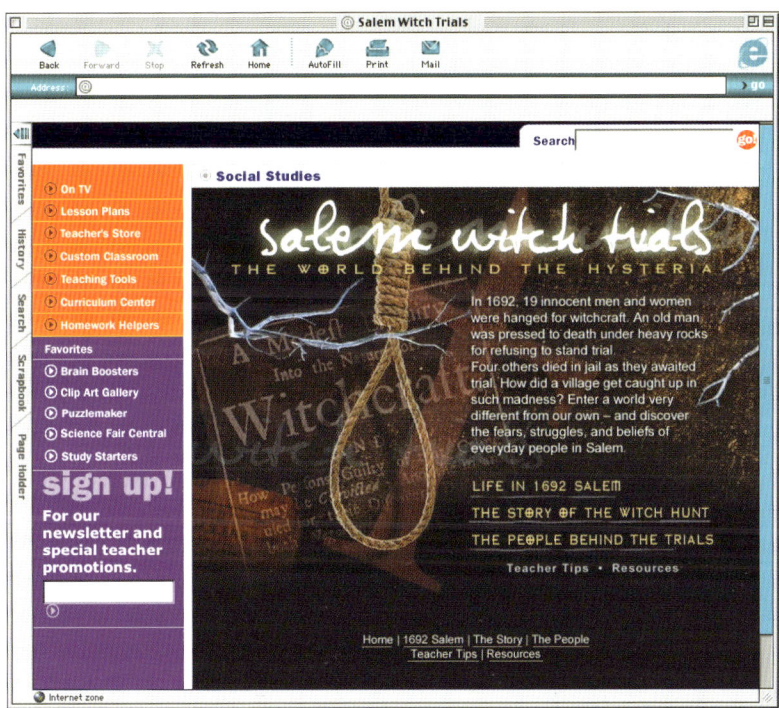

1 Below are six people of Salem who lived during the Salem witch trials. Match the descriptions (a-f) to the people (1-6).

a. A rich farmer. He didn't believe the young girls who accused people of witchcraft.
b. He was a strong believer in witchcraft and a respected minister who wrote about many religious topics.
c. A slave who was brought to Salem by the Reverend Samuel Parris.
d. A Puritan mother of seven children who was accused of witchcraft.
e. A homeless woman, one of the first to be accused of witchcraft.
f. Leader of the "bewitched" girls, she accused 62 people of witchcraft and years later apologized for her accusations.

1. ☐ Cotton Mather
2. ☐ Anne Putnam
3. ☐ Tituba
4. ☐ Sarah Good
5. ☐ John Proctor
6. ☐ Mary Easty

2 Class discussion

a. Why do you think that mostly women were accused of witchcraft?
b. Do you think witch-hunts still happen in our society?
c. Think of some groups of people who are discriminated against today.

The Birthmark[1]

1. **birthmark** : an unusual mark on the body at birth.

ACTIVITIES

Before you read

1 Fill in the gaps using the words in the box below.

> during   shape   who   strange   after
> on   past   of   started   charm   almost
> another   fairy   passion

1 .... the last part of the eighteenth century there lived a man 2 .... science. One day he left his laboratory because he had found a beautiful young woman 3 .... became his wife. Aylmer loved his young wife very much, but his real 4 .... was science and the mysteries of Nature.

One day, very soon 5 .... their marriage, Aylmer stared at his wife with a worried expression.

"Georgiana," he said, "did you know that the mark 6 .... your cheek can be eliminated?"

"No, I didn't," she said smiling. "People have called it a charm and I believed it."

"Perhaps on 7 .... face it could be a 8 ...., but not on yours. No, dearest Georgiana, your beauty is 9 .... perfect. But I hate that birthmark."

"You hate it!" exclaimed Georgiana, who 10 .... crying. "Then why did you marry me? You cannot love me if you hate my birthmark!"

In the center of Georgiana's left cheek there was a 11 .... red mark. It had the 12 .... of a very tiny human hand. In the 13 .... young men had liked the tiny hand. They said a 14 .... had put her tiny hand on her beautiful cheek. Some envious young women said that it destroyed Georgiana's beauty.

 Now listen to the first part of the story to check your answers.

PART **ONE**

A Beautiful Young Woman

During the last part of the eighteenth century there lived a man of science. One day he left his laboratory because he had found a beautiful young woman who became his wife. Aylmer loved his young wife very much, but his real passion was science and the mysteries of Nature.

One day, very soon after their marriage, Aylmer stared at his wife with a worried expression.

"Georgiana," he said, "did you know that the mark on your cheek can be eliminated?"

Stories of *Suspense*

"No, I didn't," she said smiling. "People have called it a charm,[1] and I believed it."

"Perhaps on another face it could be a charm, but not on yours. No, dearest Georgiana, your beauty is almost perfect. But I hate that birthmark."

"You hate it!" exclaimed Georgiana, who started crying. "Then why did you marry me? You cannot love me if you hate my birthmark!"

In the center of Georgiana's left cheek there was a strange red mark. It had the shape of a very tiny human hand. In the past young men had liked the tiny hand. They said a fairy[2] had put her tiny hand on her beautiful cheek. Some envious young women said that it destroyed Georgiana's beauty.

Before their marriage Aylmer did not think about the birthmark. But now it had become a frightening obsession. Georgiana's beauty was almost perfect and he could not tolerate this defect. It was an imperfection of Nature. It was Nature's way of showing that we are only mortals.

Their happiness was ruined by this birthmark. When Aylmer woke up in the morning and opened his eyes, the first thing he saw was Georgiana's crimson[3] mark. When they sat together by the fire in the evening, his eyes always looked at the birthmark on Georgiana's cheek. It was the mark of her imperfection.

END

1. **charm** : an attractive quality which brings good luck.
2. **fairy** :
3. **crimson** : dark red.

Georgiana shuddered [1] when Aylmer looked at her. And the pink color of her cheeks turned white and the little red hand became more evident. It looked like a red ruby on a white stone.

Late one night Georgiana said, "My dear Aylmer, do you remember anything about a dream you had last night — a dream about this horrible little hand?"

"No, I don't!" replied Aylmer, who was surprised. But then he added coldly, "Maybe I did dream about it, because before sleeping I thought about the hand."

"And you dreamed about it," continued Georgiana, who was almost crying. "It was a terrible dream. How can you forget it? How can you forget this sentence: 'It is in her heart now and we must take it out!' Do you remember the dream?"

Aylmer now remembered his dream. He dreamed that he was with his servant Aminadab. He was trying to remove the red birthmark. But as his knife went deeper into the cheek, the little hand went deeper and deeper. At last the little hand caught Georgiana's heart and Aylmer wanted to cut it away.

When he remembered the dream clearly, Aylmer felt ashamed. The truth often comes out in our dreams. Until now he did not realize that the birthmark had had a terrible influence on him.

"Aylmer," continued Georgiana seriously, "What can we do to eliminate this birthmark? Maybe it will cause a deformity, or perhaps the mark is as deep as life. But can we eliminate it forever?"

---

1. **shuddered** : shook with fear, trembled.

The BIRTHMARK

"Dearest Georgiana, I have thought about this a lot. And I am sure it can be eliminated."

"Oh, then please do it! I am not afraid of the risk because life with this birthmark is awful. Either eliminate it or take my life! You are a great man of science. All the world knows you. I am certain that you can do it. Please save me from madness."

"My dear wife," cried Aylmer, "don't worry. I have thought about this problem very much. I am certain that I can make your cheek as perfect as the other. I know I can correct this error of Nature and my happiness will be great."

"Then the problem is solved," said Georgiana.

Her husband kissed her right cheek which was perfect.

The next day Aylmer told his wife about his plan. "We will both live in the apartment which I used as a laboratory when I was young."

He had made important discoveries in that laboratory, and he had learned about the mysteries of Nature and the universe. Georgiana was frightened when Aylmer took her to the apartment. He looked at her happily, but the birthmark on her white cheek made him shudder and Georgiana fainted.[1]

"Aminadab! Aminadab!" shouted Aylmer violently.

A short, robust man with long hair came out of another room. This strange man had been Aylmer's assistant for many years. He did not understand scientific principles but he followed instructions and did his job well.

"Georgiana has fainted! Quickly, open the door and burn a special candle," cried Aylmer.

---

1. **fainted** : lost consciousness.

"Yes, master," answered Aminadab, looking at poor Georgiana. Then he said to himself, "He should never eliminate that birthmark!"

Aylmer was at his wife's side when she woke up.

"Where am I? Ah, I remember," said Georgiana quietly. And she put her hand over her cheek to hide the terrible mark from her husband's eyes.

"Don't be afraid, dear Georgiana," he said. "It will be a pleasure to remove it."

"Oh, please, do not look at it again. I can never forget that terrible shudder."

To help Georgiana forget her problem, Aylmer tried to entertain her. He showed her a little plant that grew slowly before her eyes. When a lovely flower appeared Georgiana exclaimed, "It's magic! I won't touch it."

"No, you can touch it! Pick the flower and enjoy its perfume."

But when Georgiana touched the flower the plant died immediately and its leaves became black.

Then Aylmer decided to create her portrait on a piece of metal. He used a scientific process that he had invented. The result was frightening because the portrait was difficult to see, but the birthmark was clearly visible. Aylmer was angry and threw the piece of metal away.

He soon forgot these failures and continued studying science and making experiments. He often went to Georgiana and told her about the mysteries of science and about the history of alchemy. He told her that science could do many incredible things. And it could easily remove the little hand from her cheek.

The BIRTHMARK

When Aylmer mentioned the birthmark Georgiana was always very unhappy.

Aylmer worked many hours in his laboratory with the help of Aminadab. One day he showed his wife a small crystal ball.

"What is this?" asked Georgiana, looking at the small crystal ball with a gold-colored liquid. "It is very beautiful. It looks like the potion of life."

"In one sense it is. It is the potion of immortality. It can prolong life or destroy life."

"Why do you keep such a terrible potion?" asked Georgiana in horror.

"Oh, don't worry, dearest Georgiana," replied Aylmer. "Look at this powerful cosmetic for the skin."

"Are you going to use it on my cheek?" asked Georgiana.

"Oh, no. Your cheek needs something that will go deeper, much deeper."

When she looked in the mirror and saw the red birthmark, she hated it more than anything.

ACTIVITIES

Go back to the text

PET 1 Look at the sentences below about Part One. Decide if each sentence is correct or incorrect. If it is correct, write A as your answer. If it is not correct, write B as your answer.

1. Aylmer's only passion in life was science.
2. The birthmark on Georgiana's cheek was shaped like a diamond.
3. Aylmer thought Georgiana's birthmark was a charm.
4. Aylmer had a dream the previous night about Georgiana's birthmark.
5. In Aylmer's dream, he cut Georgiana's cheek with a knife.
6. Aylmer told Georgiana that her birthmark could not be removed.
7. Georgiana didn't want Aylmer to remove her birthmark.
8. Aminadab didn't know much about the sciences.
9. Aminadab thought it was a good idea to eliminate the birthmark.
10. When Georgiana touched the flower, it died and its leaves turned black.
11. Aylmer created a beautiful portrait of Georgiana which didn't show her birthmark.
12. The crystal ball in Aylmer's study contained the potion of immortality.

1 ...... 2 ...... 3 ...... 4 ...... 5 ...... 6 ......
7 ...... 8 ...... 9 ...... 10 ...... 11 ...... 12 ......

ACTIVITIES

"Before sleeping, I thought about the hand"

Look at these sentences:

***Before I went out**, I changed my clothes.*

***Before going out**, I changed my clothes.*

After the words **before** and **after**, we can use a gerund.

Now look at the examples below:

*I always read the paper **before I go** to work.*

*I always read the paper **before going** to work.*

2 Rewrite the sentences below so that they have the same meaning as the first. Be sure to use before or after and a gerund in your answer.

a. Aylmer worked all night on his experiment. He was exhausted.
After ....

b. Hawthorne lived in Salem. Then he moved to Concord.
Hawthorne lived ....

c. Let's have dinner. Then we can go to a movie.
Let's have dinner ....

d. I went to sleep after I did my homework.
After ....

e. Bill worked every day for 6 months. He took a vacation afterwards.
After ....

f. I'm going to practice the piano. Then I'm going to call my friends.
Before ....

g. Aylmer gave the magic potion to a plant. Then he gave it to Georgiana.
Before ....

ACTIVITIES

3 Odd one out
Circle the word that doesn't belong in each line. Then say what the three remaining words have in common.

1. stare   look   eye   see
2. clearly   angry   slowly   immediately
3. terrible   incredible   passion   perfect
4. happiness   imperfection   immortality   failure
5. beautiful   young   deformity   perfect
6. cheek   eye   skin   heart
7. crystal ball   potion   charm   knife
8. faint   shudder   hide   worried
9. coldly   frightened   seriously   happily

Now put the words into the correct place in the table below.

nouns	adjectives	verbs	adverbs

4 Look at the picture on page 44 and answer the questions below.

a. Where are the two people in the picture?
b. Describe how they are dressed.
c. How do you think the woman is feeling?
d. What is the man thinking about the woman?
e. What impression does this picture give you?

ACTIVITIES

Before you read

 1 Listen to the beginning of Part Two and answer the questions below.

  a. What was the most interesting book in Aylmer's library?
  b. What did it contain?
  c. Why did Georgiana cry when she read this book?
  d. What did Georgiana forget to tell Aylmer?
  e. What was the first thing Georgiana saw when she entered Aylmer's laboratory?
  f. How did Aylmer look when he was preparing the potion?
  g. Why was Aylmer angry with Georgiana?
  h. What, according to Georgiana, was the only danger?
  i. What did Aylmer tell Georgiana to do?
  j. Why did Aylmer want Georgiana to be perfect?

Now read Part Two and check your answers.

2 Look at the title of Part Two, "Perfection is Dangerous". What do you think this means? What could the dangers be for Aylmer and Georgiana?

PART TWO

Perfection is Dangerous

While Aylmer worked in his laboratory, Georgiana looked at the books in his library. There were books by scientists, poets and philosophers. But the most interesting work was a big book written by her husband, in which he wrote down every experiment of his scientific career.

The book was the history of his intense and ambitious life. As Georgiana read it she loved Aylmer more and more. She knew he was a great scientist. However, many of his experiments were failures. And this made her very sad. One day she put her face on the open book and started crying.

The BIRTHMARK

When Aylmer entered the room and saw her he said, "It is dangerous to read a wizard's books."

"Now that I have read this book I adore you more than ever," said Georgiana.

"Ah, but wait for THIS success," he said, "and then adore me if you want. But now I would like to hear your beautiful voice. Please sing to me, my dearest."

So Georgiana sang and Aylmer was very pleased. Then he returned to his laboratory. But Georgiana had forgotten to tell her husband about a strange sensation she had felt on her left cheek for the last two or three hours. So she entered into her husband's laboratory for the first time.

The first thing she noticed was the furnace with its intense fire. All around the room there were tubes, cylinders and other scientific instruments. The air was filled with strange vapors and odors. But what really surprised her was Aylmer himself. He was as pale as death and worried as he prepared a strange new potion. He was so different from the man she had seen a few moments before!

"Carefully, Aminadab, carefully!" he cried. "This is a very important moment."

"Ho! Ho!" said Aminadab. "Look, master, look!"

Aylmer raised his eyes quickly and became very angry when he saw Georgiana. He went to her and took her arm.

"Why did you come here? Don't you trust [1] your husband?" he cried angrily. "Now go away!"

"No, Aylmer," said Georgiana firmly. "You don't trust me and you don't tell me your worries about this experiment. I will accept all the risks."

---

1. **trust** : believe in, have confidence in.

Stories of Suspense

"No, no, Georgiana," said Aylmer impatiently.

"I will drink any potion you give me. I trust you completely."

"My dear wife," said Aylmer, "you must know that this red hand is deep inside you. There could be danger."

"Danger? There is only one danger — that this horrible birthmark remains on my cheek," cried Georgiana. "Remove it, remove it, or we will both go mad."

"Your words are very true," said Aylmer sadly. "And now, please go back to your rooms. The potion will soon be tested."

When Georgiana returned to her rooms she thought about Aylmer's noble character and his great love for her. He wanted her to be perfect because he loved her so much.

Her thoughts were interrupted by Aylmer's footsteps. He carried a glass with a bright, colorless, transparent liquid. He was pale but didn't seem worried or afraid.

"This potion is perfect," he said looking at Georgiana. "It cannot fail."

"My dearest Aylmer, life has become very difficult. I think death is the best solution for me."

"But why do you speak of death? The potion cannot fail. Look at its effect on this plant."

Near the window there was an old geranium plant. Its leaves were yellow and ugly. Aylmer poured a small quantity of the potion in the plant. After a short time the ugly yellow leaves became green.

"I did not need any proof," said Georgiana quietly. "I believe you. Give me the potion. I am happy to drink it."

"Drink then, my dearest wife. Soon your body will be as perfect as your spirit."

The BIRTHMARK

Georgiana drank the potion and gave Aylmer the empty glass.

"It is like water from a magic fountain. Now, dearest Aylmer, let me sleep."

She fell asleep almost immediately. Aylmer sat by her side and watched her very carefully. He often looked at the birthmark on her white cheek. At first it was very visible. Then it slowly disappeared.

"It's almost gone!" said Aylmer to himself. "Success! Success! But Georgiana is so pale!"

He heard his servant laugh. He too was delighted.

Aylmer looked at Aminadab and said, "You served me well. Heaven and earth have done their part. The experiment is a success, Aminadab!"

These exclamations disturbed Georgiana's sleep. She opened her eyes and looked in the mirror. She smiled weakly when she saw that the little red hand had almost disappeared. Then she looked at Aylmer. She was worried.

"My poor Aylmer," she said quietly.

"Poor? No! I am the richest and happiest man! And you are my splendid wife! Now you are perfect!"

"My poor Aylmer," she repeated lovingly. "You have done your best. Your intention was very noble, but now I am dying."

It was true! The fatal hand was linked to Georgiana's life. When it disappeared, Georgiana's life disappeared too. And so she died.

Aylmer had wanted perfection but he did not realize that perfection was not part of this world. And so he lost the woman he loved and destroyed his happiness forever.

ACTIVITIES

Go back to the text

1 Put the events of Part Two in the correct order. The first one has been done for you.

- **a.** ☐ Georgiana drank the potion and fell asleep immediately.
- **b.** ☐ Georgiana entered Aylmer's laboratory for the first time.
- **c.** ☐ Georgiana looked in the mirror and saw that her birthmark had nearly disappeared.
- **d.** ☐ Aylmer sent Georgiana back to her room.
- **e.** ☐ Georgiana died.
- **f.** ☐ Aylmer warned Georgiana about the dangers of removing the little hand.
- **g.** ☐ 1 Georgiana read Aylmer's book.
- **h.** ☐ Aylmer gave some of the potion to an old geranium plant and its leaves became green.

PET 2 This is part of a letter you receive from your penfriend.

> Have you ever read any books about witches or wizards? My favorite books are the *Lord of the Rings* trilogy. Have you read them?

Now write a letter to your penfriend to tell him/her about the books you have read on witches or wizards. If you haven't read any, tell him/her about your favorite book.

Write your letter in about 100 words.

ACTIVITIES

T: GRADE 5

3 Topic — Work

In the story, Aylmer worked as a scientist. What kind of work would you like to do? Talk to the class about the kind of work you'd like to do. Bring in a photo of someone doing this kind of work, and use these questions to help you.

a. What is your ideal kind of work?
b. Why did you choose it?
c. Which is more interesting, the work you have chosen or Aylmer's?
d. Will it be easy for you to find work when you finish your studies?

4 Look at the words from the story in the table below. Write the definition in the space provided in your own words (use a dictionary to help you if you need to).

Word	Definition
a. furnace	
b. laboratory	
c. passion	
d. charm	
e. wizard	
f. envious	
g. imperfection	
h. potion	
i. eliminate	
j. fatal	
k. portrait	
l. proof	

ACTIVITIES

5 Now complete the sentences below using words from the table on page 61.

a. Aylmer painted a .... of his wife.
b. There was a/an .... accident in the laboratory. The .... exploded.
c. Many women were .... of Georgiana's beauty. They weren't as beautiful as she was.
d. I always carry a "rabbit's foot" wherever I go. It's my good luck ....
e. The scientists went back to work in their .... after the meeting.
f. Georgiana kissed Aylmer with a lot of .... She really loved her husband.
g. There are too many candidates for the job. We'll have to .... some of them.
h. Aylmer thought Georgiana's birthmark was a sign of her .... He wanted to remove it.
i. The .... made a magic .... from strange ingredients.
j. Georgiana didn't need any .... that Aylmer could eliminate her birthmark. She trusted him.

6 Let's talk about the story.
Answer the questions below in your own words, then ask your classmates what they think.

a. Do you think people's appearance is important? If so, why?
b. Do you think Georgiana was right to want to remove her birthmark?
c. Find out what this phrase means: "Don't judge a book by its cover." Is there a similar expression in your language? Do you agree with it?

The magic
of alchemy

Alchemy was an ancient art that was half magic and half science. Before the 18th century when important discoveries were made, it was very difficult to separate science and magic and people often confused the two.

People who studied alchemy wanted to turn common metals such as copper, zinc, lead or tin into gold or silver. They thought that by combining certain elements they could produce the "philosopher's stone", which would make ordinary metals into gold, considered the

An alchemist (17th century) by David Teniers the Younger.

perfect metal. Their other goal ¹ was to discover the secret of life. Alchemists wanted to discover a magic potion that could prolong life or make life eternal.

However, through their experiments alchemists learned about different materials and how they reacted together. The important discoveries that alchemists made helped form the modern science of chemistry.

Alchemy began in China and Egypt about 300 BC and by 700 AD it reached the Middle East. During the Middle Ages (1100s and 1200s) it reached Western Europe.

Alchemy had a religious aspect too. Alchemists believed that their work could make them better individuals. Alchemists used magic-looking symbols to write down their experiments. Each symbol represented a chemical substance.

Alchemy and astrology became closely related. Alchemists believed that the sun, the moon and the planets represented and controlled certain metals. An alchemist's laboratory was a mysterious, exciting and dangerous place to work. It was full of glass containers with strange substances, fires and red-hot metals!

In the 1200s the medieval alchemist Roger Bacon invented gunpowder. ² This was a very important invention that changed the way people made war.

One of the most famous alchemists was a Swiss doctor called Paracelsus (1493-1541). He was one of the first doctors to use chemistry in medicine. He traveled to the Middle East and looked for an element that could change metals into gold. At that time alchemists believed that gold could become a miraculous medicine.

Sir Isaac Newton (1642-1727) was probably the greatest scientist of

1. **goal** : purpose.
2. **gunpowder** : an explosive powder used in guns.

his time. He made important discoveries in the field of physics. He too was interested in alchemy. He followed alchemists' experiments and contributed his own original ideas to the theories of alchemy.

The ancient art of alchemy came to an end in the 18th century because of the developments of chemistry and science. In the 1780s Antoine Lavoisier explained that when an object burned it mixed with oxygen. No one had ever known this before. His research was the beginning of the science of modern chemistry.

The Alchemist from a German book on the Philosopher's Stone (1582).

1 Answer the questions below.

   a. What was alchemy?
   b. Why was it hard to separate science and magic before the 18th century?
   c. What were the two main goals of alchemy?
   d. Where did alchemy begin?
   e. What did alchemists believe about the planets?
   f. What did Roger Bacon invent?
   g. How did the art of alchemy come to an end?
   h. Whose research was the beginning of modern chemistry?

2 Complete the table below with information from the text.

Name	Known for...	When?	Other information
Roger Bacon		1200s	
	One of the first doctors to use chemistry in the field of medicine		
	Discoveries in physics... contributed original ideas to alchemy		
		1780s	

3 How important is chemistry today? Make a list of all the things around you (and on you!) that are the result of chemical research. Then compare your list with your classmates'.

Dr Heidegger's *Experiment*

ACTIVITIES

Before you read

1 Fill in the gaps using the words in the box below.

> seclusion   killed   misfortune   forgotten   unusual   health
> dishonest   gentlemen   transaction   merchant   invited

Dr Heidegger was a very ¹ .... old man. One afternoon he ² .... four friends to meet him in his study. There were three very old ³ ...., Mr Medbourne, Colonel Killigrew and Mr Gascoigne. And there was a very old lady called Widow Wycherly. They were all very sad people who had been unfortunate in life. However, their biggest ⁴ .... was their age.

When Mr Medbourne was young he was a rich ⁵ .... But he had lost everything during a bad business ⁶ .... Now he was very poor.

Colonel Killigrew had thrown away his best years, his ⁷ .... and his money in sinful pleasures. Now his mind and body were tormented.

Mr Gascoigne had been a bad man and a ⁸ .... politician. Fortunately, time had passed and people had ⁹ .... him.

Widow Wycherly had been a great beauty when she was young. But for many years now she had lived in ¹⁰ .... and solitude because of certain terrible stories about her. During their youth, each of the three gentlemen had been in love with Widow Wycherly. They had almost ¹¹ .... each other for the woman they loved.

   Now listen to the beginning of Part One to check your answers.

68

PART **ONE**

Dr Heidegger's Friends

Dr Heidegger was a very unusual old man. One afternoon he invited four friends to meet him in his study. There were three very old gentlemen, Mr Medbourne, Colonel Killigrew and Mr Gascoigne. And there was a very old lady called Widow [1] Wycherly. They were all very sad people who had been unfortunate in life. However, their biggest misfortune was their age.

1. **widow**: a woman whose husband has died.

Stories of Suspense

When Mr Medbourne was young he was a rich merchant. But he had lost everything during a bad business transaction. Now he was very poor.

Colonel Killigrew had thrown away his best years, his health and his money in sinful pleasures. Now his mind and body were tormented.

Mr Gascoigne had been a bad man and a dishonest politician. Fortunately, time had passed and people had forgotten him.

Widow Wycherly had been a great beauty when she was young. But for many years now she had lived in seclusion and solitude because of certain terrible stories about her. During their youth, each of the three gentlemen had been in love with Widow Wycherly. They had almost killed each other for the woman they loved.

"My dear friends," Dr Heidegger said, "please sit down. I would like you to observe a little experiment."

Dr Heidegger's study was an unusual place. It was a dark, old room with cobwebs.[1] On the walls there were bookcases with many important books. On one bookcase there was a statue of Hippocrates. People said that Dr Heidegger talked to Hippocrates when he had a difficult medical problem to solve.

In a dark corner of the study, inside a small closet, there was a human skeleton. Between the two bookcases there was a tall mirror. People also said that the doctor's dead patients looked at him from this mirror. On the opposite side of the room there was a big portrait of a young lady dressed in a magnificent dress. When the doctor was young he loved her and wanted to marry

1. **cobwebs** :

Dr Heidegger's EXPERIMENT

her. But on the evening before their marriage he gave her the wrong medicine and she died!

The most curious thing in the doctor's study was a big black book without any title. It was a book of magic. Once when a servant had tried to touch it, the skeleton moved in the closet, the portrait of the young girl moved on the wall and many frightening faces appeared in the mirror.

A small round table stood in the middle of the doctor's study. On the small table there was a beautiful vase. There were also four champagne glasses on the table.

"My dear old friends," said the doctor, "please help me with this experiment."

Now, we must remember that Dr Heidegger was a very strange old gentleman.

When the doctor's four friends heard him talk about this experiment, they thought to themselves, "Oh, we will probably examine a cobweb under the microscope or some similar nonsense." But this time Dr Heidegger entered the study with the black book of magic. He opened it and took out an old rose which had been in the book for many years.

"This rose," he said, "is fifty-five years old. It was given to me by Sylvia Ward, whose portrait is on the wall. I wanted to wear it at our wedding. I have kept it in this book for fifty-five years. Now, do you think this rose can blossom[1] again?"

"What nonsense!" exclaimed Widow Wycherly. "Can an old woman's face be young again?"

"Please look at this," said Dr Heidegger.

---

1. **blossom** : (here) become fresh.

Stories of Suspense

He uncovered the vase and threw the rose into the water it contained. At first nothing happened. Then there was a change. The old, brown rose began to change color — it became red. And its leaves became green. The rose was suddenly fresh and beautiful.

The doctor's friends were indifferent because they had seen better experiments at the doctor's study.

"Well, how did you do it?" one of them asked.

"Did you ever hear of the Fountain of Youth?" asked Dr Heidegger. "The Spanish explorer Ponce de Leon looked for it two or three centuries ago."

"Did he ever find it?" asked Widow Wycherly.

"No, because he didn't look in the right place. The famous Fountain of Youth is in the southern part of Florida. A friend of mine sent me the water you see in this vase."

Colonel Killigrew did not believe a word of the story and asked, "What does this water do to the human body?"

"You will soon see," replied Dr Heidegger. "All of you are welcome to drink this water. Drink as much as you need to be young again!" He paused for a moment and then said, "I will not take part in this experiment because I do not want to become young again. I will only observe the experiment."

ACTIVITIES

Go back to the text

1 **Answer the questions below.**

a. What was the biggest misfortune of Dr Heidegger's friends?
b. Why did Mr Medbourne, Mr Gascoigne and Colonel Killigrew almost kill each other?
c. What was Dr Heidegger's study like?
d. What happened to the young lady that Dr Heidegger loved?
e. What was Dr Heidegger's book about? What happened when a servant touched it?
f. Who gave Dr Heidegger the rose?
g. Who didn't believe the story about the rose?
h. Where is the Fountain of Youth? Who looked for it?
i. Who sent Dr Heidegger the water?
j. Why didn't Dr Heidegger want to take part in the experiment?

2 **Fill in the table below with information about Dr Heidegger's friends.**

Person	What did he/she do in the past?	What is he/she like now?
Mr Medbourne		
Colonel Killigrew		
Mr Gascoigne		
Widow Wycherly		

ACTIVITIES

3 a. Tell your partner everything you can remember about Dr Heidegger's study.

b. Now complete the description of Dr Heidegger's study using the prepositions from the box below (they can be used more than once).

in   inside   on   of   at

There were bookcases [1] .... the walls with many important books. [2] .... one bookcase there was a statue of Hippocrates. [3] .... a dark corner of the study, [4] .... the closet, there was a human skeleton. [5] .... the other end of the room there was a portrait of a beautiful woman. [6] .... the middle [7] .... the study there was a small round table. There was a beautiful vase and four champagne glasses [8] .... the table.

4 Find the words from Part One in the square below. Use the definitions on page 77 to help you.

ACTIVITIES

a. Bad luck (10).
b. Extremely unhappy, like Colonel Killigrew (9).
c. Being alone (8).
d. A woman whose husband has died (5).
e. A place where you keep things (6).
f. You use it to get better if you are sick (8).
g. We all have this under our skin (8).
h. A spider's home (6).
i. You use it to put flowers in (4).
j. The .... of Youth (8).

5 Noun or adjective?
Fill in the table below with the corresponding noun or adjective.

	Noun	Adjective
a.	youth	
b.		dishonest
c.		beautiful
d.		sad
e.	sin	
f.	health	
g.		famous
h.	similarity	
i.		dead
j.	color	

ACTIVITIES

PET 6 Look at these sentences. For each question, complete the second sentence so that it means the same as the first. Use no more than three words.

1. The rose was given to Dr Heidegger by Sylvia Ward.
   Sylvia Ward .... the rose.

2. "I think the rose will blossom again," said Dr Heidegger.
   Dr Heidegger said he thought the rose .... again.

3. "We will never make the same errors again."
   "We promise .... the same errors again."

4. "My friend sent me the water in this vase."
   "A friend of .... sent me the water in this vase."

5. I've had this black book of magic since 1850.
   I've had this black book of magic .... fifty years.

6. Widow Wycherly was very beautiful when she was young.
   During .... Widow Wycherly was very beautiful.

7. If they don't drink the water of youth, Dr Heidegger's friends won't look younger again.
   Dr Heidegger's friends won't look younger unless .... the water of youth again.

8. Why don't you drink some water from the Fountain of Youth?
   If I were you, ... drink some water from the Fountain of Youth.

ACTIVITIES

Before you read

PET 1 Listen to the beginning of Part Two. Decide if each sentence is correct or incorrect. If it is correct, put a tick (✓) in the box under A for YES. If it is not correct, put a tick in the box under B for NO.

		A YES	B NO
1	The water from the Fountain of Youth smelled very bad.	☐	☐
2	Dr Heidegger's friends didn't believe in the water's magic powers.	☐	☐
3	Dr Heidegger's friends didn't notice any changes after drinking the youth water.	☐	☐
4	Dr Heidegger told his friends to be patient.	☐	☐
5	There was enough water for half of the old people in the city.	☐	☐
6	After Colonel Killigrew told Widow Wycherly she was beautiful, she ran to the mirror to look.	☐	☐
7	After drinking some water, the three men felt tired and weak.	☐	☐
8	Mr Gascoigne began to talk excitedly about business.	☐	☐
9	Colonel Killigrew sang a happy song.	☐	☐
10	Colonel Killigrew did not think Widow Wycherly was attractive.	☐	☐

Now read the text and correct the incorrect sentences.

PART **TWO**

The Fountain of Youth

Dr Heidegger filled the four champagne glasses with the water of the Fountain of Youth. The water was effervescent and had a pleasant perfume. The four friends decided to drink it although they did not believe in its magic powers.

Dr Heidegger looked at his friends and said, "Before you drink this water, remember the errors you made in your youth and do not repeat them. Now you are all old and you have learned from your errors."

The four friends laughed but did not say anything. "We have experience now and we will never make the same errors again," they thought.

Dr Heidegger's EXPERIMENT

"Please drink, then!" said the doctor.

With trembling hands they drank the water of youth. What a sad spectacle to watch! They were old and gray, and there was no life in their decrepit bodies.

Suddenly, a healthy color appeared on their gray cheeks. They looked at one another and saw that something was happening. They were slowly changing!

"Give us more of that magic water," they cried happily.

"We are younger now — but we are still too old! Give us more!" cried Mr Gascoigne.

"Yes, give us more, more!" cried Mr Medbourne.

"Be patient," said Dr Heidegger who was watching the experiment carefully. "It took you a long time to become old and decrepit. You certainly can wait thirty minutes to become young again."

He filled their glasses with more of the water of youth. In the vase there was lots of water for half of the old people in the city. The doctor's friends quickly drank their second glass. After a short time their eyes became happy and their white hair became darker. And now there were three middle-aged gentlemen and an attractive middle-aged woman sitting around the table.

"My dear widow, you are lovely!" cried Colonel Killigrew who was watching the changes on her face.

However, the widow knew that Colonel Killigrew's compliments were not always true. So she ran to the mirror to look at herself. "I hope I don't see an ugly old woman in the mirror," she thought to herself.

The three gentlemen suddenly were exuberant. They felt excited, young and full of energy.

Stories of Suspense

Mr Gascoigne's mind began thinking about political matters. He started talking excitedly about patriotism and national glory. He was still a politician.

Colonel Killigrew started singing a happy song while he admired Widow Wycherly's young, attractive body. He still liked the pleasures of life.

Mr Medbourne was working on a new business transaction. He wanted to sell ice to the East Indies! "What a clever idea!" he thought. "I can use whales [1] to transport the ice from the polar region to the East Indies." He was busy calculating dollars and cents. He was still a merchant.

Widow Wycherly stood in front of the mirror and looked at herself — she was very surprised! Her face had become young and beautiful. Then she put her face close to the mirror to examine the color of her hair which had become dark. "Now I can take off the cap [2] I always wear to hide my white hair," she thought. She felt very young and attractive, and even talked to the lovely image in the mirror. Then she went back to the table happily.

"My dear old doctor," she cried, "please give me another glass of the water of youth."

"Certainly," replied the doctor. "I have already filled the other glasses too."

It was almost evening and it was getting dark in the study, but the vase with the water of youth shone with [3] its own light.

1. **whales** :
2. **cap** : soft, flat hat.
3. **shone with** : (shine, shone, shone) gave out, radiated.

Dr Heidegger's EXPERIMENT

Dr Heidegger sat in a big chair with a mysterious look on his face. After drinking the third glass the four friends were much younger. All the problems and illnesses of old age were forgotten. They felt like new people.

"We are young! We are young!" cried one of the gentlemen.

Now that they were young again they laughed at their old clothes. One of them walked slowly across the room like a decrepit old man and the others laughed. Another put on a pair of glasses and looked at the black book of magic and again the others laughed. The third friend sat on a chair and imitated Dr Heidegger. Then they all jumped happily around the room.

Widow Wycherly, who was now a beautiful young lady, said, "Doctor, come and dance with me!" The four young people laughed louder than ever.

"Please excuse me, but I am old and I have rheumatism. I certainly cannot dance. But I am sure one of these young gentlemen will be happy to dance with you."

"Oh, dance with me, Clara," cried Colonel Killigrew.

"No, no. I will dance with Clara," shouted Mr Gascoigne.

"Clara promised to marry me fifty years ago! I will dance with her!" said Mr Medbourne.

They all formed a circle around Clara. One gentleman took both her hands passionately and another embraced her.[1] The third put his hand under her cap and touched her hair.

There was never a better picture of young rivalry. (However, people said that the tall mirror on the wall showed the figures of three old, gray men fighting over an ugly old woman.)

---

1. **embraced her** : held her in his arms as a sign of love or affection.

Stories of Suspense

The four friends were young and full of passions. All three of the young gentlemen wanted the attention and the love of the young lady. The three rivals began to fight violently and became dangerous. As they fought, the small round table fell over. The vase with the water of youth fell over and broke. The precious water of the Fountain of Youth was all over the floor.

"Gentlemen! Madam Wycherly! Stop this fighting! Stop it immediately!" cried the doctor.

They stopped fighting and looked at Dr Heidegger who was sitting in his chair holding Sylvia's rose. Then they sat down because they were very tired.

"My poor rose," said Dr Heidegger, "it is dying again."

As the four young friends looked at the rose it became dry and brown.

"But I still love it," he said and kissed it.

His friends trembled. They felt a strange sensation in their bodies and spirits. What was happening to them?

"Are we becoming old again?" one of them asked.

Yes, they were becoming old again. The water of youth had had a very short effect.

The old widow put her hands in front of her face. She was very unhappy.

"Yes, my friends, you are old again," said Dr Heidegger, "and the water of youth is all over the floor. But I am not sorry because I don't want to drink it. I don't want to become young again. You have taught me an important lesson."

But the doctor's friends did not agree with him. They decided to travel to Florida and drink from the Fountain of Youth at all hours of the day and night.

ACTIVITIES

Go back to the text

1 Choose the correct answer (a, b, c or d) to the questions below.

1. Dr Heidegger told his friends that they had learned from
   a. ☐ their errors.
   b. ☐ their teachers.
   c. ☐ their parents.
   d. ☐ their studies.

2. What happened after the friends drank the first glass of water?
   a. ☐ They felt ill.
   b. ☐ They wanted more.
   c. ☐ They started fighting.
   d. ☐ They fell asleep.

3. What did the three men fight about?
   a. ☐ They wanted the water of youth.
   b. ☐ They disagreed about political matters.
   c. ☐ They wanted to dance with the widow.
   d. ☐ One of them insulted the other two.

4. Which phrase is *not* true about Dr Heidegger's friends?
   a. ☐ One of them imitated Dr Heidegger.
   b. ☐ They forgot about their old age.
   c. ☐ They laughed at their old clothes.
   d. ☐ One of them drank more water while the others weren't looking.

5. After drinking the third glass of water, what happened to Dr Heidegger's friends?
   a. ☐ They forgot about their problems and their old age.
   b. ☐ They were drunk.
   c. ☐ They returned home.
   d. ☐ They went to Florida.

ACTIVITIES

6. What happened to the vase containing the water of youth?
   a. ☐ It was stolen.
   b. ☐ It fell on the floor and broke.
   c. ☐ Someone drank all of the water it contained.
   d. ☐ It was forgotten by everyone.

7. What happened when the rose started dying?
   a. ☐ Dr Heidegger became very angry.
   b. ☐ Dr Heidegger's friends became old again.
   c. ☐ Dr Heidegger gave it more of the water of youth.
   d. ☐ Widow Wycherly gave Dr Heidegger a new one.

8. Why wasn't Dr Heidegger sorry?
   a. ☐ Because he knew where the Fountain of Youth was.
   b. ☐ Because he didn't like his friends.
   c. ☐ Because he knew he will die soon.
   d. ☐ Because he didn't want to drink the water of youth.

9. What did the doctor's friends decide to do at the end of the story?
   a. ☐ travel to Florida to drink from the Fountain of Youth
   b. ☐ celebrate being young
   c. ☐ convince Dr Heidegger to drink from the Fountain of Youth
   d. ☐ convince other people to drink the water of youth

10. What do you think is the moral of this story?
    a. ☐ Don't drink strange water.
    b. ☐ Don't believe in legends.
    c. ☐ Old people are always happy.
    d. ☐ Be happy with how you are.

ACTIVITIES

2 **Who said what?**
Match the quotes below (a-m) about Part Two with the speakers (1-5).
Be careful — these are not all direct quotes from the story!

a. ☐ Remember the mistakes you made in the past.
b. ☐ It took a long time to get old.
c. ☐ You're beautiful, Widow Wycherly!
d. ☐ I hope I don't see an ugly old woman in the mirror!
e. ☐ I can bring ice from the polar region to the East Indies using whales.
f. ☐ Now I can take off my cap!
g. ☐ Could I have another glass of the water of youth?
h. ☐ I am sure one of these young gentlemen will dance with you.
i. ☐ Clara, will you dance with me?
j. ☐ I want to dance with the widow!
k. ☐ Clara said she would marry me fifty years ago.
l. ☐ Stop fighting, all of you!
m. ☐ I learned an important lesson from you.

1. Dr Heidegger
2. Colonel Killigrew
3. Widow Wycherly
4. Mr Medbourne
5. Mr Gascoigne

ACTIVITIES

"They looked at one another and saw that something was happening"

We use the Past Continuous to talk about a particular moment in the past. Look at the example below:
*Last night at 9 p.m. I **was watching** TV.*

was/were + the -ing form of the verb

We often use the Past Continuous and Past Simple in the same sentence. Look at the example below:
*I **was eating** dinner when the phone **rang**.*

We use the Past Continuous for the action which was in the middle of happening and the Past Simple for the sudden completed action.

3 When Dr Heidegger's friends drank the water of youth, some strange things happened. Choose a verb from the box below and write sentences about what each character was doing at the time. Use the Past Continuous. There is one extra verb you will not need.

a. (to think) ... about politics   Mr Medbourne
b. (to sing) ... a song   Colonel Killigrew
c. (to talk) ... about patriotism   Mr Gascoigne
d. (to watch) ... his friends   Widow Wycherly
e. (to calculate) ... dollars and cents Dr Heidegger
f. (to look) ... in the mirror

a. Mr Gascoigne was thinking about politics.
b. ....
c. ....
d. ....
e. ....

ACTIVITIES

T: GRADE 5

4 Topic — Friends

We have just met four of Dr Heidegger's friends. Do you have an interesting friend?

Talk about one of your friends to the class. Bring in a photo of one of your friends and use these questions to help you.

a. How long have you known this person?
b. How did you meet?
c. What activities do you like doing together?
d. Why is your friend important to you?
e. Has your friend ever taught you anything?

5 Let's talk about the story.

Answer the questions below in your own words, then ask your classmates what they think.

a. Have you heard the expression "the grass is greener on the other side?" If you don't know already, try to find out what it means. Is there a similar expression in your language?
b. Why do you think some people aren't happy in their present situations?
c. Why do you think Dr Heidegger's friends wanted to become young again? What did they find difficult about being old, in your opinion?
d. How are old people treated in your country? Do the young take care of the old?

EXIT TEST

1 Choose the correct answer (a, b, c or d) to the questions below.

1. What was the nature of all people, according to the dark figure in "Young Goodman Brown"?
   - a. ☐ greed
   - b. ☐ good
   - c. ☐ happiness
   - d. ☐ evil

2. What did Goodman Brown's companion look like?
   - a. ☐ his brother
   - b. ☐ his father
   - c. ☐ his grandfather
   - d. ☐ his uncle

3. What was Goodman Brown's resolution for the future?
   - a. ☐ I will stay close to Faith.
   - b. ☐ I won't walk in forests anymore.
   - c. ☐ I will be nice to everyone I meet.
   - d. ☐ I won't do anything evil.

4. Aylmer's real passion in life was science and
   - a. ☐ his wife.
   - b. ☐ plants.
   - c. ☐ alchemy.
   - d. ☐ the mysteries of nature.

5. Where was Georgiana's birthmark?
   - a. ☐ on her right cheek
   - b. ☐ on her left cheek
   - c. ☐ on her nose
   - d. ☐ on her forehead

EXIT TEST

6. Before giving Georgiana the potion, what did Aylmer do?
   a. ☐ He poured some on a plant to see its effects.
   b. ☐ He drank some himself.
   c. ☐ He gave some to Aminadab.
   d. ☐ He wrote in his book.

7. What was in Dr Heidegger's black book of magic?
   a. ☐ An old rose.
   b. ☐ A magic formula.
   c. ☐ Old newspaper articles.
   d. ☐ Short stories.

8. Which one of Dr Heidegger's friends was interested in politics?
   a. ☐ Colonel Killigrew
   b. ☐ Widow Wycherly
   c. ☐ Mr Gascoigne
   d. ☐ Mr Medbourne

9. Who did Widow Wycherly ask to dance with her?
   a. ☐ Colonel Killigrew.
   b. ☐ Mr Gascoigne.
   c. ☐ Mr Medbourne.
   d. ☐ Dr Heidegger.

10. Which statement is *not* true about Nathaniel Hawthorne?
    a. ☐ He was very interested in his Puritan ancestors.
    b. ☐ He was interested in the legends of Salem.
    c. ☐ He had two children.
    d. ☐ He attended Bowdoin College.

11. Which scientist or inventor invented gunpowder?
    a. ☐ Paracelsus
    b. ☐ Roger Bacon
    c. ☐ Antoine Lavoisier
    d. ☐ Sir Isaac Newton

EXIT TEST

PET 2 Look at these sentences. For each question, complete the second sentence so that it means the same as the first. Use no more than three words.

1 I have a friend. She lives in Salem, Massachusetts.

   I have a friend .... in Salem, Massachusetts.

2 Goodman Brown was walking through the forest. He heard people chanting.

   Goodman Brown heard people chanting .... through the forest.

3 Widow Wycherly drank the water of youth. Then she looked in the mirror.

   Before .... the mirror, Widow Wycherly drank the water of youth.

4 People accused the governor's wife of being a witch.

   The governor's wife .... being a witch.

5 While I was on vacation I read many books about alchemy.

   During .... I read many books about alchemy.

6 Dr Heidegger is the only one who doesn't want to become young again.

   Everyone wants to become .... Dr Heidegger.

7 Nathaniel Hawthorne wrote many short stories during his career.

   Nathaniel Hawthorne wrote .... short stories during his career.

EXIT TEST

PET 3 Read the text below about *The Witches of Eastwick* and choose the correct word (A, B, C or D) for each space.

The Witches of Eastwick is a movie based **(1)** .... a novel by John Updike. On Thursday nights three female friends — Alex (Cher), Sukie (Michelle Pfeiffer) and Jane (Susan Sarandon) — meet to relax, learn Chinese aphrodisiac cooking and **(2)** .... about finding men who are single. As they sit around, they **(3)** .... their idea of the ideal male.

Arriving in town the following day is the devil, in the shape **(4)** .... the mysterious stranger Darrell Van Horn (played by Jack Nicholson), **(5)** .... tries to seduce each of the women. Then, strange things start happening. **(6)** .... the town matriarch Felicia publicly denounces Van Horne, she suddenly gets a fracture. When she **(7)** .... her husband to publish a story about Van Horne's actions, Darrell gets **(8)** .... revenge with revoltingly large amounts of cherries. The women realize **(9)** .... they may be in danger and begin planning their escape.

Jack Nicholson gives a wonderful performance in this extremely **(10)** .... movie.

1	A on	B about	C of	D for
2	A talking	B talked	C talks	D talk
3	A describe	B describes	C describing	D described
4	A for	B by	C of	D to
5	A who	B who's	C whose	D which
6	A During	B For	C When	D However
7	A says	B makes	C says	D orders
8	A her	B his	C their	D theirs
9	A who	B that	C which	D whose
10	A best	B wonderful	C great	D funny

EXIT TEST

4 Do you remember...

Guess the question word for each question using the words from the box below. Then answer the questions.

who   what   where   why

1. .... was Hawthorne born?
2. .... did Goodman Brown's companion look like?
3. .... was Goodman Brown's catechism teacher?
4. .... did Goodman Brown hide in the forest?
5. .... was Georgiana's birthmark?
6. .... was Aylmer's assistant?
7. .... was Aylmer's dream about?
8. .... was the Fountain of Youth?
9. .... was the "dishonest politician"?
10. .... did Dr Heidegger use a rose for?
11. .... did Dr Heidegger's friends go to Florida?

Key to Exit Test

1 1. d 2. b 3. a 4. d 5. b
   6. a 7. a 8. c 9. d 10. c 11. b

2 1 who lives 2 as he walked 3 looking in / she looked in 4 was accused of 5 my/the vacation 6 young again except 7 a lot of

3 1 A 2 D 3 A 4 C 5 A 6 C 7 D 8 B 9 B 10 D

4 1. Where ... Salem, Massachusetts. 2. Who ... Goodman Brown. 3. Who... Goody Cloyse. 4. Why ... He was afraid and heard the sound of horses. 5. Where ... On her left cheek. 6. Who ... Aminadab. 7. What ... About the tiny hand on Georgiana's cheek. 8. Where ... in Florida. 9. Who ... Mr Gascoigne. 10. What ... To show what the water of youth could do. 11. Why ... To visit the Fountain of Youth and drink the water.